WEALTH MENTALITY

WEALTH

MENTALITY

 WEALTH MENTALITY

INDEX

10 distinctive differences of the rich from the poor

The rich believe they create their own destiny, while the poor believe they are predestined

The rich have big dreams while the poor dream small

The rich commit themselves to their dreams, while the poor sleep dreaming their dreams

The rich play to win while the poor play just to avoid losing money

Rich people connect with rich and successful people, while poor people connect with poor people.

Rich people learn well, while poor people think they know everything.

Rich people are leaders while poor people are followers

Rich people focus on saving while poor people focus on spending

Rich people have their money working hard for them, while poor people work hard for their money

Summary

The 4 Essential Wealth Skills

Wealth Ability 1: Making money from scratch

Richability 2: Budgeting Your Money

Richability 3: Making more money with money

Wealth Ability 4: Protecting Your Money

7 Vital Steps to Change Your Tomorrow, Starting Today

Conclusion

WEALTH MENTALITY

10 distinctive differences of the rich from the poor

A lot of people think life is very unfair. He is working hard here, yet his income is not even enough to buy him ice cream. On the other side of the coin, you know someone who doesn't even spill a drop of sweat and yet lies in luxury. If you think that life has been so rude to you and that you were born to suffer your fate, you are thinking as a poor man would think. But if you believe that you are the master of your destiny and have total control of your life, then you have the mentality of a rich man.

Knowing the well-kept secrets of millionaires

WEALTH MENTALITY

is the key to opening the door to success. In most cases, wealthy people will tell you that there is no exact formula for being well in life. The secret lies in the attitude that facilitates the flow of wealth. The focus is on the psychological aspect of rich people.

In today's society, the gap between rich and poor is widening every day. The rich become richer while the poor become poorer. To help us understand the satirical situation, we need to deepen the mentality of the rich and blessed and compare it with the thinking of the poor and disadvantaged. Here are the ten different differences in the monetary mentality of the rich versus the poor. As you read the differences, try to evaluate your own mentality and see where yours mainly belongs.

But remember that in defining "rich" and "poor" I am not referring to the size of the current bank account, net worth, assets, etc. But rather, I am referring to the state of mind. A human mind is so powerful that it can create assets, or even liabilities. If you have a mind conditioned to be poor, no matter what wealth you have today, you may lose it sooner or later. On the other hand, if you have the mind of a rich person, you can create your wealth from scratch or recover it faster than it took you the first time, even if you lose everything today.

WEALTH MENTALITY

The rich believe they create their own destiny, while the poor believe they are predestined

Destiny refers to the predetermined course of events in one's life. The idea of destiny has a deep history and divine intervention is the most popular belief. People trust that their lives depend on the will of a supernatural being. All actions are in vain if they do not coincide with the will of the divine.

- Destiny VS action

 WEALTH MENTALITY

Rich people

Rich people create an incredible life because they don't believe in the predetermined destiny. Instead, they believe that life is what they do. If you rest all day and wait for the big fruit to fall into your mouth, nothing will move. Everything will remain in place unless you move it. Like Newton's Law of Motion, "unless a net external force acts, a resting body remains at rest and a moving body remains in motion. This scientific example is true even in real life and rich people apply this theory in their lives. For rich people, they believe they are responsible for their own lives. They create their own destiny and not the economy, luck or knowledge.

 WEALTH MENTALITY

Poor people

The poor, on the other hand, believe they are slaves to their own destiny. Whatever they do, adversaries come no matter how they elude them.

- In control VS out of control

Poor people

The poor believe they live a rebellious life. Their existence is very uncontrollable. When they act, the results are always unmanageable. When they fail in their efforts, they blame the economy, the boss, their family and others who were not in consequence.

 WEALTH MENTALITY

Rich people

The rich think otherwise. Life is a series of plans. With the right planning and the right actions, the results are favorable. They take full responsibility for all their actions.

Conclusion:

When you keep thinking that life only happens to you, you will eventually lose the power to change things and control your life. A rich man takes responsibility for the circumstances he created, while a poor man feels like a victim of the world. If you want to reach financial abundance, think like a rich man would. Believe that you create your future and not other people or events.

The rich focus on opportunities, while the poor focus on problems.

Opportunities come directly and indirectly. Problems mask possibilities. When you look at things superficially, you only see the façade and you don't appreciate the blessing underneath.

- Opportunities VS obstacles

Poor people

The difference between rich and poor is the attitude towards a problem. When faced with a problem, a poor man sees it as an obstacle to his easy life. He hates hardship and sees it as an obstacle to his relaxed life. The more problems he faces, the more he sees his life as complicated.

Rich people

The rich see the problem as a door to new opportunities. They focus on the solution rather than wasting time in despair. With each obstacle, they treat things positively and look beyond the obvious. The rich concentrate on finding solutions to their crisis. They elucidate things to see things from a better perspective.

- Action VS complaint

 WEALTH MENTALITY

Poor people

The poor continue to complain about obstacles. They waste time complaining about the circumstances of their lives. At the end of the day, their complaint intensifies as they have done nothing to solve the problem.

Rich people

The rich act on their problems. They may moan a little, but they work to unravel misery. The more problems they solve, the better their feelings.

Conclusion:

Problems and failures are part of your molding process to become difficult and a better person. With problems, you learn from your mistakes and improve when the next one arrives. When faced with an opportunity, creative solutions come to mind. Avoid the poor man's action of sitting down and getting in a bad mood about it.

WEALTH MENTALITY

The rich have big dreams while the poor dream small

Dreaming is the motivation for success. When a person dreams, he strives to achieve his dreams. Both rich and poor dream. The difference is the size of your dream. When you have small dreams, you work less while big dreamers work more to achieve their vision.

- Large VS Small

Poor people

The poor have little dreams. They dream of eating three times a day, having a small house to live in and getting a good paying job. These are all the dreams of a poor man. Because any casual employee can easily do it, many poor people feel they don't need to work harder. Why work harder anyway? They have achieved their dream after all.

Rich people

For rich people, to achieve great things, you have to dream big. Rich men stick to this principle. They don't dream of eating three times a day, they dream of eating more than that in luxury. They do not dream of a small house, they dream of a comfortable house for their family plus a house to rest during their holidays. They do not dream of a job with good pay. Instead, they create jobs.

- Aspirant VS satisfaction

Poor people

The poor are content with what they have. They do not aspire to more. They believe that wanting more means complicating your life. When poor people achieve their little dreams, they begin to live a life of poor quality.

Rich people

The rich aspire to more. They believe their

skills can take them to places. Because they have big dreams, they work hard to turn aspirations into reality.

Conclusion:

You can't achieve bigger things if you only have small dreams. When you dream, you dream big, anyway, there's nothing to lose in dreaming.

The rich commit themselves to their dreams, while the poor sleep dreaming their dreams

It's a fact that dreams are the first step to success. But it doesn't end there. For dreams to come true, you must work for them.

- Commitment VS dreaming

 WEALTH MENTALITY

Poor people

Poor people love to dream even when the sun is high. They stay in a good mood even when it's time to work. They keep dreaming that things will happen in an instant. They still think how good it is to live in opulence, but never do anything to experience it.

Rich people

The rich work hard on their dreams. They commit every day of their lives to achieve their goals. They pool their efforts to build the life of their dreams.

Conclusion:

Dreaming big doesn't make you rich. You need to work hard when you set your goals. Small steps every day are better than just waiting for time to pass without action. At the end of the day, small actions can accumulate and take you to the ladders of success.

WEALTH MENTALITY

The rich play to win while the poor play just to avoid losing money

The big difference in mentality is the purpose of playing the game. Life is a bet. Every decision is a risk. There is no certainty in this world.

- Risk taking VS play safe

Poor people

The poor play the game of life just to avoid losing. They are too careful to invest and make sure things go the way they want. In case of doubt, they never make a decision. They always stay safe. They remain attached to the stigma of failure and too afraid to make mistakes.

Rich people

For the rich, life is about taking risks. Because they know exactly what they want, they invest to earn. For them, losing is never an option, they study and analyze how things work and invest once they know the flow of things.

Conclusion:

Only those who are willing to take risks achieve financial stability and abundance.

 WEALTH MENTALITY

The greater the risk you run, the greater your reward. However, even rich people don't take risks without preparation. When you go out on a limb, make sure your preparation is sufficient to guarantee victory. Be armed when you play with life.

 WEALTH MENTALITY

Rich people connect with rich and successful people, while poor people connect with poor people.

The people around them have an indirect effect on our ways of thinking. Try to associate with pessimistic people and eventually you will be pessimistic. However, when you go to a company of jovial people, you absorb their joy.

- Receptivity VS hostility

 WEALTH MENTALITY

Poor people

The poor are hostile to the rich. They think their lifestyle is not tolerable. Instead, they associate with people with the same income as their own. They spend their time wondering how rich people become richer and envy the fate they have.

Rich people

The rich are receptive to new ideas and new people. They spend time with people who can help them achieve their dreams. They join people who earn six digits or more. They analyze how these rich people become richer and absorb their forms and thoughts.

Conclusion:

The poor think that their wealth depends on the origin of their family. You are rich if you only belong to a rich family. The rich think the opposite. They go with people who can help them. They talk to financially successful people by taking notes on their secrets to prosperity. With the right associations, you can get rich even if you come from a poor family.

 WEALTH MENTALITY

Rich people learn well, while poor people think they know everything.

Life is about learning. When you declare that, you know everything, learning stops. However, when he admits that he still needs more knowledge, he will long to learn more.

- Open-minded vs. closed-mindedness

Poor people

The poor think they know everything. They know how life works and how to live well.

Their beliefs make them close their minds to new ideas. If you are not willing to learn, you will never know why rich people become richer and why they remain poor despite all their efforts.

Rich People

The rich admit they still need to learn. When you give it room for improvement and new ideas, you open your mind to the possibilities. One of the easiest ways to get financial abundance is to learn from people who achieved status.

Conclusion:

The key to financial success is to accept your

shortcomings and learn from people. To be the best, you need to learn from the best and learn to be the best. Only when you open yourself to learning can you live a life of abundance.

Rich people are leaders while poor people are followers

Most financially successful people lead the way. As a leader, you are at the forefront of action. Because of the courage needed to be a leader, only those with strong personality become the manager.

- Leaders VS followers

Poor people

The poor have a herd mentality. They like to

follow where the water flows. Instead of taking the initiative, they are happy to let others think. They don't want to take responsibility for their decisions. When someone asks for their opinion, they pass it on to others so as not to be blamed for the failures later on.

Rich people

The rich take the initiative. They decide for themselves and take full responsibility for their decisions. They can work independently.

Conclusion:

The rich are leaders and the leaders are rich.

This idea arises because of the independent attitude of leaders and rich people. Even if it is an ordinary office, leaders are often responsible for the whole group. They may have greater responsibilities, but they also receive higher salaries.

WEALTH MENTALITY

Rich people focus on saving while poor people focus on spending

No matter how small or large your profit, saving is a crucial part of getting rich. If you try to save even ten dollars a day, that means 3,650 dollars a year and 36,500 in ten years. Well, that's even less interest you get from the bank. Even if you earn $100,000 a month but also spend the full amount, you'll never get rich until you die.

- Savings vs. spending

Poor people

Poor people usually spend more than they earn. They don't believe in the value of saving. They make $100 and spend $110. Over time, overspending builds up and before you know it, you are drowning in debt.

Rich people

Wealthy people stay on a monthly or even daily budget. They spend only within their stated budget. They save a portion of their earnings in the bank to earn more interest.

- Debit card VS credit card

 WEALTH MENTALITY

Poor people

The poor depend on credit cards. They cannot live without them. They dine shop and go on holiday with their plastic cards. Because they don't see the expenses and their cash remains intact, they feel they have total control of their finances. Only to discover later that everything is getting out of control.

Rich people

Rich people don't buy with credit cards. If they don't have cash, they use debit cards. They believe in the saying, "If you can't pay it in cash, you can't really pay it.

- Cautious VS Impulsive

Poor people

The poor are impulsive buyers. They buy anything on offer and anything at a discount. Even if they don't need the items, they keep buying thinking they can save off the discounts.

Rich People

The rich think about the product many times before they buy it. They consider the affordability, quality and usefulness of the item. When an item fails one of the criteria, they think repeatedly before finally deciding.

 WEALTH MENTALITY

Conclusion:

Making money is difficult. Because of the difficulty in earning it, think twice or even three times before letting go of your hard-earned income. No one knows the future, so it's important to save to make sure you have something in case of drought.

Rich people have their money working hard for them, while poor people work hard for their money

Everybody works hard. The way to let your money work for you is to know where to invest it. If you know where to put your investments, it will make your money work hard for you.

- Successful investment VS useless investment

 WEALTH MENTALITY

Poor people

The poor are still looking for money to come. They continue to work and work to earn. They spend beyond their means and resort to interest-bearing loans.

Rich people

The rich know where to invest their money. Instead of banks charging them for credit card interest, they charge interest on their savings. They experience a quiet life while their money works for them.

Conclusion:

To stop working hard for your money like poor people do, live within your means and save. Let your money do the work and enjoy life.

Summary

You can't blame anyone born into a poor family. Maybe you can call that fate. But to die even as poor as rats, you only blame yourself. On average, a man lives for 70 years. The approximately 25,550 days of your life are enough to make you rich. If you waste your days, fate should not be the reason why you remained poor for the rest of your life.

The millionaires' secret is easy. They take each day as a new beginning to face the challenges that will help them achieve their big dreams. Complaining is a total waste of time. Instead of comparing yourself to others, they work on their own lives. They take

initiative rather than mere follow-up. They trust their knowledge and skills and are not afraid to take the risk.

Despite the situation of destitution that surrounds us, money is plentiful. You can see money everywhere. You are in the wrong place at the wrong time. To take advantage of prosperity, be in the right place at the right time. Act. Find opportunities to get rich.

Where can you classify yourself? Do you have a rich mentality or do negativities dominate your mind? Getting rich is very simple.

All you need is the right attitude, mentality and action. With these characteristics, embarking on the long, winding road to

 WEALTH MENTALITY

wealth is just one step away. Adapt the mentality of the rich and be rich; otherwise, stay poor with the habits and mentality of the poor.

The 4 Essential Wealth Skills

It's probably silly to ask people who want to be millionaires. Without the need for further study and research, the answer will be a resounding yes. Earning more than you need and spending on the things you not only need but also on the things you want are luxurious dreams for many. It's everyone's dream to trot around the world, send children to prestigious universities, indulge in pampering, and donate to charities to help the poor. Enjoying all this seems like a distant ambition.

Everyone wants to be a millionaire. But the

key to being one of the richest men in the world is knowing the essentials to give you all the luck you need. While there is no exact formula for wealth, there are keys that will help you open the doors to success. It comes down to an effective system applied by the rich and rich. This should probably be very effective for them to live in the luxury and grandchildren of their children. Using the same skills won't make you lose anything. Anyway, yes, you eat three times a day, but you barely fit into your family's trivial income.

Before presenting the essential wealth skills, it's appropriate to prepare him for his journey to prosperity. As in any effort, you must prepare and arm yourself with anticipated needs. As you trot along the path of financial abundance, you must get organized. These are the important things you should carry with you as you move forward on the path to success.

Vision

The beginning of financial wealth is the vision you must establish. As your vision becomes bigger, your likelihood of becoming a millionaire is also greater. What's to lose anyway? To count the countless millions in your hands, you need to visualize yourself with your hands on your fortune. Do you want a car, two or three? Do you want to have a successful business or an international business with branches all over the world? Think and imagine what your power can accommodate. Focus on the positive outcome of things and envision a comfortable and financially abundant life for yourself and your family. If you believe this will happen, it will. Otherwise, your doubts will keep you stationary.

Plan

Rich people don't just dream. They plan things and they do it specifically. They have a plan every day and stick to it. They consider each day as a day to contribute to their future success. You just can't leave your life to luck or how the poor see it, to destiny. Millionaires do not believe in predetermined destiny. Instead, they take responsibility for their lives. They are in perfect control of their destiny. Instead of sitting down, they write down all their goals and make a systematic wealth plan that they follow religiously.

Understanding

In order for you to reach your goal and establish plans, you must understand your whole situation. Look at your state from a broader perspective. Millionaires understand the flow of many into their hands. They know how much comes in and how much they should let go. The poor just try to balance this flow. Sometimes the exit is even greater than the entrance. But for millionaires, their cash output is less than their cash income. Therefore, they can save from their profits.

Commitment

To become a millionaire, you must commit to your dreams. Making millions takes a lot of

 WEALTH MENTALITY

effort and commitment. Remember, the road to financial abundance is not an easy one. There will be countless obstacles. If you have little commitment to your dream, you can quickly give up when you stumble.

These are the essential things that you must carry with you along the road to millions. If you're ready to take a major turn in your life, read on to learn the secrets of those who sleep in luxury. Be ready to evaluate your own life and take steps to make a change. As you read the article, you'll be surprised to learn that all you need to have are four wealth skills and you're ready to begin the journey to prosperity. Now, let's see if you can get to the end of the road.

WEALTH MENTALITY

Wealth Ability 1: Making money from scratch

It can be quite skeptical to become a millionaire from scratch. But it's true. Many rich men started out of nothing.

Unlike other people who have a thick checkbook, abundant savings and many properties to liquidate to start a business, you probably think you'll never be a candidate to become a millionaire. However, you don't need all of this. All you need is yourself. You are the greatest and most indispensable asset of your future business. There are many known ways to make money from scratch. If you think this is impossible, look around.

 WEALTH MENTALITY

Most successful people started from scratch. All you need to do is let your imagination work, be creative and have confidence.

1. Selling

Garage Sale

Selling is the traditional way to make money from scratch. You can sell your products, especially your second-hand items, trash or other odds. Instead of storing the items in your warehouse, you can turn them into cash. When you do this, you'll be one to say, "There's money in the trash.

Real Estate

If you have good communication skills, then you have the power to convince people with your words and your words can be your best asset. Many successful real estate entrepreneurs started from scratch. With only their voice and words as initial capital, they were able to create millions.

Getting Started

In addition to real estate, you can also sell other people's products. You can offer to sell their products along with yours. In return, you can get a commission for each item sold.

Selling gives you an unlimited source of

 WEALTH MENTALITY

funds. As long as you are hard-working in dealing with different people, it is a sure success. However, since you work in a customer-related environment, be sure to be very patient. You'll meet people with varied personalities who will test your character. But don't get involved. Keep in mind that they can be your potential key to success.

If you like to sell, you should always be on the move. If your business requires it, it must be where the action is. Flexibility of time is very important as many customers don't want to wait and there are many competitors who yearn to win as much as you do. While it may seem like a difficult start, you will get the fruit of your efforts by creating a name for yourself. When that happens, you can be the boss of your own company.

2. Offer your service

Each person has a unique ability to offer. The secret to making money from scratch is to take advantage of its uniqueness. You can stand out from the crowd when you show off your exceptional skill, talent or ability. To turn your skill into cash, offer your service to others. Advertise and keep your customers satisfied to ensure that customers repeat or are referred by others. Aside from the usual forms of advertising, don't forget to charm people. Millionaires have a certain charm that attracts people to them. As you bring more people closer to your services, your own company will have a multi-million dollar value in no time.

Providing services is not just easy money. It also serves as an outlet for your talents, skills

and abilities. Remember, you weren't here to keep your uniqueness inside. You have to share it with the world and make it known. Not only does it improve you, it also benefits other people.

The idea is to look for customer problems and find a solution to those problems. If people worry about broken things, fix them. As long as you find a solution to your most common problems and needs, you will never lose your commercial market.

3. Go online!

With the advent of online business, you don't need to leave your own comforts just to earn a six-figure income. You can earn money from home as long as you have access to the

Internet. When you're online, the chances of making money from scratch are endless. The money is right under your nose and just a click away. The good thing about working online is that you stay at home without bosses and still earn better than those who work within the boundaries of their office. Here are the common jobs to make money online.

Blogging Online

Online blogging started as a people hobby. It was their way out of their everyday emotions and feelings. However, as people relate to their own stories, they acquire followers who contribute to their blogs. As your blogs increase in number, visitors come and interact with you. When online advertisers see the increase in traffic to your site, they

start asking for an ad space, and this can be your chance to earn income from something that started as a hobby.

Article Writing

People use the Internet as their primary source of information. This is why online marketers require a great deal of information to satisfy most online search engines. However, not everyone has the time and talent to write and this is where you can get in. You can write for someone and get paid for it.

Making money from scratch is difficult. Your capital is just you. However, don't worry; you have the best starting capital that even big companies don't have. By investing a

WEALTH MENTALITY

large amount of money, you also risk a lot. However, when you start from scratch, you have nothing to lose and a lot to gain. It can be quite challenging, but the rewards are rewarding. If you want your first million now, you can have it right away. It's your own pace and no one will dictate how much or how much you can earn.

WEALTH MENTALITY

Richability 2: Budgeting Your Money

In the first part of the article, you mentioned about understanding your money. If you want to be a millionaire, you must learn wealth skill number two, budget your money. The rich don't spend more than they earn. Instead, they religiously keep a part of it and let it earn interest. To follow in his footsteps, he learns to manage his finances. Unless you learn this important skill, you will never reach the path to financial abundance.

The Importance of Budgeting Your Money

Provides ideas

Budgeting your money gives you knowledge of your profits and expenses. When you have a basic knowledge of the whereabouts of your money, you create financial stability, which is the crucial step toward abundance.

Teach self-control

When you know how to budget your money, you develop self-discipline. You can control your finances and avoid unnecessary expenses. Learning to budget makes you the boss of your money rather than a slave to your finances.

 WEALTH MENTALITY

Organize Your Finances

Organizing your finances warns you of any potential financial problems. Your budget can serve as a record of all your financial transactions, guide you to paying utility bills, and immediately warns you when you overspend.

Offer new opportunities

When you know how to budget your money, you can take advantage of opportunities you might otherwise miss. Because you know the flow of money, you can determine exactly if you have surplus funds to invest in other opportunities to make money.

Providing More Cash Flow

The biggest benefit of budgeting your money is having extra money. When you cut unnecessary payments such as penalties and late interest, you can save for your future needs. When you pay your bills on time, not only do you avoid late fees, but you also create a good name for yourself and your business.

Earning your first million is a challenge, and budgeting according to your needs is more challenging. The key to being rich is having control of your finances.

Knowing the benefits of budgeting is useless if you don't practice it. To arm yourself with the necessary competence in wealth skill

number 2, here are some tips to help you stay within your budget.

Tips for budgeting your money

Make a list

When you receive your first million, get in the habit of making a list of things you must pay. Determine your future expenses and set aside funds for your needs. If you run a business, be sure to separate your company's work budget. These include money for the purchase, maintenance and salary of your employees. If you don't have a company and only work for yourself or others, know your expenses until the next payday. Write down each item specifically, and in front of each item, its corresponding amount. That way, you'll know if you're still within your budget or if you're exceeding your profits.

Spread Your Money

For people who are very impulsive when it comes to spending, it is ideal to split the budget into parts. You can allocate your funds as follows:

- Work budget

Your work budget includes your daily or monthly expenses. This usually takes up most of the budget. This is where you'll get your monthly bills, food, subsidy, and transportation paid.

WEALTH MENTALITY

- Saving

No matter how small your income, savings should be part of your budget. Being rich means saving more than you spend. Even a working poor can get rich as long as they save enough for their future. Savings should comprise at least 20% to 30% of your monthly budget.

- Spending money

Of course, life will be boring if you only work to live and save. Your monthly leisure activities should be part of your budget. As the cliché goes, "All work without play makes a child boring. Working is more rewarding and fun if you treat yourself once in a while. He can get the money for his new clothes, vacation or pamper himself with the money he spends. To avoid overspending, be sure to leave your debit and credit cards at home and stay strictly within your spending money.

WEALTH MENTALITY

Richability 3: Making more money with money

Once you have your millions, you can get richer by sitting comfortably at home and letting your money do the work. Millionaires are richer not because they work hard to earn their millions but because they let their money work hard for them. If you are on your way to financial abundance, these are the proven ways to let your money do the work for you.

Investing

Investing is the smartest way to make your

money work. However, a smart investment is important to keep your money running. Before investing, make sure you have the knowledge of the field in which you want to invest. Invest in properties that are appreciated in time such as real estate and stocks. Don't invest in appliances, electronics or even cars. These things depreciate over time. This means that instead of making more money with your money, you will end up with less.

Save on Banks

If you have an additional amount of money, you can deposit it at banks. You can keep it safe and earn interest at the same time. Although the interest isn't much, at least it earns in comparison when you keep it in your home. Other banks may give up to 3%

annual interest. Time deposits earn more compared to an ordinary savings account. The disadvantage of a time deposit is that you must allow your investment to mature before you can withdraw your money.

Offering Loans

Many people and small businesses need money to start their own business or reach the end of their financial status. When you help these people with their financial needs, you can charge them interest. Only be careful when making loans to people. Make sure they have the ability to pay to guarantee the return of your money, or better yet, ask for guarantees.

Wealth Ability 4: Protecting Your Money

Once you have the millions, know how to budget and keeps the money working for you, the next thing you need to do is protect your money. Protecting your money is important for you and your grandchildren to enjoy a luxurious life. Without adequate protection, you can be a millionaire one day and live in poverty the next.

I'm sure

Insurance protects your investments and money. Just like insuring your home and other assets, it protects your property from misfortune. When you invest your money, keep it in banks with good insurance policies. Most banks guarantee deposits of up to $100,000 per person. At that amount, it's a good idea to spread your money out at many banks to get the best out of insurance. Insurance is not only true to your money in banks, but also to your other assets.

Be a wise investor

Your millions are you're hard earned. It is the fruit of their precious time and effort. So, before you invest your money, understand the market where you will place it. A prudent investor conducts an investigation of the entry and exit of the business. He can make direct observation or work with a person known to be an expert in the field.

Conclusion:

The road to wealth is challenging. However, if you have the four essential wealth skills, everything will be easy. Remember, you can make money from scratch, but once you have it, learn how to budget your money, make it work for you, and protect it. Although wealth doesn't come overnight, you can start adapting and mastering skills now. The sooner you start the skill, the sooner you'll get rich.

 WEALTH MENTALITY

7 Vital Steps to Change Your Tomorrow, Starting Today

The future is a manifestation of present facts. You can know your future by your present actions. You can transform your future by changing your present life. However, change is one of the most difficult things to experience. Many people cannot tolerate drastic changes in their lives. Because of the uncertainties that come with change, people are reluctant to change. If you want to change your tomorrow, you must begin the changes today. Here are the 7 vital steps to help you bring a more fruitful tomorrow.

1. You are the sum of the 5 people you spend most of your time with

If you want to know your future, look at the lives of the people you are currently with. The people around you have a direct influence on your life. You acquire some of their attitudes, principles and practices. You are like a small child who absorbs the practices of the adults around him. When you go with dishonest people, you eventually alter your own values and acquire their dishonesty. However, if you go for honest people, their honesty reinforces your own personal values. The kinds of people you share your life with are very powerful personalities who affect your current actions and later own your future life. Because of their great impact on your life, it is very important that you know them well. Once you know their influence on you, you will know how to take advantage of it.

The idea of being the sum of the people around you is often one of the most forgotten parts of human psychology. Although this is not a novel thought, people continue to ignore the influence of others in their lives. As a result, they end up being their detested character. All this is because they spent too much time with the person. The person he is with can lift him up as much as he can knock him down. The first step in changing your future today is to meet the five people in your inner circle. So that you can see their impact on your life, these are the steps you can take.

Identify the five people you spend most of your time with

Since you are the sum of the people around you, you must be careful about the people you spend most of your time with. Although some of them are indispensable in your life, like your parents or siblings, try to spend as little time as possible with unavoidable people with a negative impact on your future life. Other people with whom you can often spend time are your friends, office or schoolmates, and your special person. Each person may have a different response to the five people they spend most of their time with. But most will revolve around these groups.

Identify the qualities of these five people

Once you have identified the five people in

WEALTH MENTALITY

your life, try to evaluate each person's personality. Look at them in every aspect of your life. Look at your family relationship, your dedication to work or school, your attitude toward problems, and your outlook on life. Getting to know these people will help you get to know yourself better.

Identify the attitudes you share with these five people in your life

After getting to know your central circle and its special attributes, try to evaluate your own life. What positive and negative characteristics do you possess? With whom can you relate your characteristics? When you are able to identify the main influence on that character trait, you can do something about it. If you want to improve a positive attribute from one of your main groups, try approaching the person. The more time you spend with him/her, the better you will be able to imitate that attitude. However, if you see mainly negative attributes for your main group, reconsider your relationship with the person better.

Everyone needs a tribe. However, your tribe must exert a good influence on your life to benefit from it. If you are in bad company, your future is at risk. Your choices today, including your choice of company, have a direct effect on your life. If you want to know your future, look at the lives of the people you spend most of your life with.

2. Find a Mentor

Everyone looks up to someone, it could be an

old teacher, your parents or an older sister or brother or your best friend. The person you admire can serve as your mentor. Because you love him, you will most likely listen to his suggestions and teachings. A good mentor provides new knowledge and leads you on the right path. If you want to change your life tomorrow, look for a good mentor who will lead you to the kind of life you want to have. To find out if your mentor is good to keep, here are the ideal characteristics of a mentor.

Act as a role model

You have to practice what you teach. To be an effective mentor, you must do what you say. The best way to lead a person in the right direction is to model a good example. As the cliché says, actions speak louder than

words. If your mentor is worthy of emulation, look at his life. Otherwise, he must find other mentors to relate his life to.

Willingness to share

A good mentor is someone who is willing to share the secrets of the good life. If your mentor is open to sharing his or her experience and teaching you the skills to succeed in life, you can trust the person with your life.

Motivate others

A good mentor can bring out a person's intrinsic motivation. For your mentor to be a good leader, he/she must bring out the best in you. Some students or followers return to their old ways when the mentor disappears. If you are one of these people, your mentor is not effective. An effective mentor naturally brings out the inner motivation of his followers. Even in your absence, followers remain within your teachings without the need for constant supervision.

3. Start or join a team of like-minded people

The effort of a group is stronger than the effort of an individual. When you want to transform your life today, join groups or teams with the same interest as yours. Unlike when you work alone to change some aspects of your life, a group effort is stronger and more difficult to disrupt. When you belong to a team, your conviction for a better life is harder and therefore more difficult to break. When you reach a saturation point, your team can help and support you throughout the journey. Unlike working alone, your like-minded team can support you when you lose your perseverance. Here are the advantages of teamwork.

Provides a sense of security

Teamwork gives you a sense of security. When you have a group that shares the same interest as yours, you are sure of their support for any problems that may arise. You know that there are people who stay with you and will guide you as you go.

 WEALTH MENTALITY

More learning

As you work with people, you increase your knowledge with their experiences. Because you share a common interest, you can draw wisdom from them. You don't have to personally experience things just to learn. By listening to their feelings, you can learn a lot from the events in their lives.

Compensate for an individual's weakness

Each person has his own weakness. When you work alone to change your future, even the slightest weakness can be detrimental to your goal. However, if you have a team, other members can compensate for their own weakness. They can help you deal with a weakness and teach you how to overcome it.

You can draw strength from the team especially in your lowest situation.

Developing a personal relationship

Joining a team also gives you relationships that are more personal. As you spend more time with your team, you can find friendship with them and influence each other. Again, in this case, we go back to the five people with whom you spend most of your time. Make sure the team you are joining will have a positive impact on your future life.

Greater understanding of other people's perspective

Because you are working with other people,

you will better understand how people think and act. You can use your learning to assess your own character and then improve your personality.

4. Entering the Business

Most people who want to transform their lives start with a business. If you realize it, the richest people are not employees, but entrepreneurs who risked doing things on their own. If you want to achieve better financial status in the future, you can start setting up your own business today. Here are the perceived benefits of owning your own business.

WEALTH MENTALITY

Be your own boss

If you are an employee, you should get along well with your boss and co-workers. There are too many people to work with. You need to adapt to their personality and whims. When you have your own business, you become your own boss. You don't have to adapt to anyone's whim. All he needs to do is work hard and work with his future clients.

Flexible time

Working in an office means spending 8 hours in the area. You cannot leave the workplace as sanctions are ready for implementation. When you have your own business, you can own your time. You have the last word on your day off, working hours and your rest

time.

Generate unlimited income

Because you work at your own pace, you can generate more income as you wish. Unlike an ordinary employee, you only receive your paychecks twice and in a set amount. In business, you can generate millions in days or years depending on your own ability.

5. Start a Bank Account for Investment Purposes

Opening a bank account helps you save your resources and invest for your purpose. Instead of having money in your hands, having a bank account brings you countless

benefits. These are the few advantages of maintaining a bank account.

Safer

When you have your bank account, you don't personally keep your money. The bank is responsible for your money. Therefore, it protects you from thieves and possible disasters such as natural and man-made calamities. Even during a bankruptcy, your money has insurance to keep the depositor worry-free.

Easier to store

Banks help you save money. Most people who overspend have more cash. When you keep your money in the banks, you avoid spending too much. You also avoid withdrawing a large amount of money at banks because of their existing withdrawal limits.

You earn interest

With bank accounts, your money works for you. If you keep your money in your own custody, the value is the same from day one until the day you need it. If you keep it in the banks, it becomes your personal investment because it earns interest every month.

6. Time management: how to get more time in a day to build your financial freedom

Sometimes you can hear people say that 24 hours in a day is not enough to finish all their work and meet all the deadlines. If you're one of these people, you'll hear answers like, "If you can't find time, take time. With the busy society you're in, you feel you need to compress everything in 24 hours. The secret to achieving your established goals is simply to stop complaining, sit down and start doing the work. Most people who keep saying that time is not enough are the people who love to complain. Instead of using work time, they spend two or three hours complaining and discerning how to start work. If others can compress all their obligations in the given time, why can't you?

Time management

The key to meeting your deadlines is through efficient time management. With the right allocation of your time and task, you can achieve your goal and still find time to relax. Although time management is a skill, you can learn it while you practice it. These are some of the proven beneficial time management tips.

Prioritize things

You can start your day by listing the things you need to accomplish by prioritizing those that are urgent. When you have a to-do list, you can keep your mind focused on your list and avoid straying from it. You can create the list by writing down those who need your immediate attention. Once you finish the most urgent one, you can start doing the next one in line and so on. By prioritizing things, you avoid sacrificing one task over another.

Know your most productive hours

Different people have different levels of productivity during the day. Although most people are more productive in the morning, there are also people who find the evenings relaxing to work the best way. If you are a morning person, try delegating complicated tasks in the morning. When you know your most productive hours, you can allocate this time to do a difficult job and reserve the easiest ones during your downtime.

 WEALTH MENTALITY

Start and finish your task

The problem with people who complain of insufficient time is to leave a task unfinished and start a new job. If you want to adapt a good time management skill, finish all the tasks you have started. Otherwise, your day will have ended with several open and pending tasks. In the end, you don't get even a small job and you will totally ruin everything.

Analyze your situation

If you feel yourself running after the clock every day, it's time to sit down and analyze the whole situation. There may be problems in the way you manage your time. Discover activities where you spend too much time.

Once you discover this, you can be more attentive in doing so. If you spend three to five hours surfing social networking sites, you can reduce this to one hour so that the remaining hours are more productive.

Create a goal

One goal is your motivation for time management. When setting your goals, be realistic. Remember that you only have 24 hours in one day. Never set goals that are not feasible. Otherwise, you will end up frustrated every day.

Delegate and subcontract

There is nothing wrong with volunteering

your services to people. However, be realistic. You can't be a hero every day. Learn how to delegate other tasks to people you trust and let them take responsibility for it. As much as you want to do everything, multi-tasking is often difficult. If you're not good at that, you'll end up sacrificing some things for others.

Use Your Waiting Time Productively

Waiting is one of the most time-consuming activities. He waits his turn at the cashier's line, waits for food service and waits for a long queue at the department store. He can spend these hours waiting productively. Instead of seeing the next page fall or the next person who will walk through the door, you can bring a good book to read or review documents or take any useful tasks with you.

As you learn to do this, the amount of work you finish during your waiting times can save you from many obligations.

Time management is learning to use your time wisely and for your own benefit. It's a skill that no one teaches you, but you must learn to survive life's challenges. As long as you keep your things well organized, you will control your time and your life.

7. Focus on one project at a time!

Our brains are like computers. When you do several tasks at the same time, the computer hangs up and breaks down. Like computers, our brain can only completely accommodate one project at a time. Although some people believe in multitasking, the quality of the product produced from multitasking is not as efficient as the project produced with full focus. This is because your brain can only concentrate on one thought at a time. When you follow the concept of one project at a time, your production is superior and more likely to be completed.

Staying focused on one project and closing your thoughts of other tasks is quite difficult. The presence of constant distractions in the environment and in your mind can easily divert your attention to other things. No matter how difficult the skill, you must master it to create changes in your life that will be beneficial to your future. To help you learn the skill, here are some tips to follow.

Divide things into small pieces

Don't get overwhelmed with a big task. If you can divide it into smaller tasks, so much the better. Divide the difficult task into several smaller, achievable projects. Instead of getting an overwhelming project, try dividing it into divisions.

Eliminate possible distractions

You work best in a quiet environment; find a quiet room where you can concentrate on your project. Avoid distractions such as noise, interruptions, and other forms of disturbance.

Keep your goals clear

One of the best ways to stay focused on a project is to clarify its objectives. When you have clear objectives, everyone will direct every effort to achieve the objective you set. It is easier to keep you motivated when you have realistic and achievable goals.

Conclusion

Changes don't happen in an instant. To create more lasting change for your future, you must equip yourself with the skills necessary to ensure a successful future.

No matter how much you want to achieve your goals on your own, this is quite difficult. The most successful people did not achieve success on their own.

There are people around who helped them to be the person they wanted to be. If you want to change your tomorrow, start acting today and look for people who share the same feelings as you.

Visit our author page on Amazon and get more MENTES LIBRES!

http://amazon.com/author/menteslibres

If you wish, you can leave a comment on this book by clicking on the following link so that we can continue to grow! Thank you very much for your purchase!

https://www.amazon.com/dp/B08267C63W

www.ingramcontent.com/pod-product-compliance
Lightning Source LLC
Chambersburg PA
CBHW070805220526
45466CB00002B/559